296142
066

126201

| DATE DUE | | | |
|---|---|---|---|
| | | | |
| | | | |
| | | | |
| | | | |
| | | | |
| | | | |
| | | | |
| | | | |
| | | | |
| | | | |
| | | | |
| | | | |
| | | | |

WITHDRAWN

# COME, LET US REASON TOGETHER

# Books by Beryl D. Cohon

Introduction to Judaism
  *A Book for Jewish Youth*

The Prophets: Their Personalities and Teachings

Feasts of the Lord
  *A Sacred Pageant*

Judaism — In Theory and Practice

From Generation to Generation

Jacob's Well: Some Jewish Sources and Parallels to the Sermon On the Mount

Out of the Heart: Intimate Talks from a Jewish Pulpit on the Personal Issues of Life

God's Angry Men
  *A Student's Introduction to the Hebrew Prophets*

My King and My God: Intimate Talks On the Devotions of Life

Vision and Faith: Confirmation Services for Jewish Congregations

Men at the Crossroads
  *Between Jerusalem and Rome,*
  *Synagogue and Church*
  *Lives, Times and Doctrines of the Founders of Talmudic Judaism and New Testament Christianity*

Shielding The Flame
  *A Personal and Spiritual Inventory of a Liberal Rabbi*

# COME, LET US REASON TOGETHER

Sermons Presented in Days of Crisis

*by Beryl D. Cohon*

Foreword by
Abram L. Sachar
*Chancellor, Brandeis University*

BLOCH PUBLISHING COMPANY
NEW YORK

Copyright 1977
by Sally K. Cohon

296.42
C66c
126201
Sept. 1983

Library of Congress Catalog Card Number: 76-24330

Cohon, Beryl D.
  Come, Let us Reason Together.

New York, N.Y.                    Bloch Publishing Co.
7610                              7/12/76
ISBN: 0-8197-0397-4

Printed in the United States of America

Let not the parable
be a trivial matter
in your estimation.
It is like unto a king
who drops a pearl and goes
about searching for it with
a penny candle.
    With the aid of a penny candle
    a man may find his God.

        Midrash, *Shir Hashirim*

# Contents

# Foreword

*This foreword was written by Dr. Abram L. Sachar following the death of Rabbi Cohon on June 15, 1976.*

THERE was understandable initial hesitation by Rabbi
Beryl Cohon to permit publication of a selected group
of the sermons he had preached many years earlier, during
the trauma of despair in the Hitler and Holocaust years.
How relevant could such a selection be after the passage
of nearly forty years and the vast changes in the mood and
climate of succeeding generations? I confess I approached
the reading of the manuscript with affectionate misgivings,
for I shared the concern. Yet as these thoughtful messages
are carefully studied, what emerges is a passionate appeal
to faith and stamina, confidence that, however searing the
testing point, the visceral determination of man's spirit to
survive is bound to emerge. Despair is the product of a
failure in perspective. The author uses a dramatic analogy
to make his point when he refers to the breed of mice that
lived so long in the cellars of Salazar that they lost all
vision. Rabbi Cohon insists that we are not a race of blind
mice if we determine not to be, that reason and understanding can be triumphant, even at the edge of an atomic
apocalypse, if the spirit is unflagging. How much more
contemporary can such a message be, especially for the
saddened younger people who sit disconsolately on the
mourner's bench?

Of course one must not expect, in the cold pages of
print, the intensity and vitality that the preacher poured

into his message, especially when the dominant mood of disenchantment had to be fought with personal vigor. For that matter, the written word rarely reproduces the emotional climate in which it has been uttered. Missing are the nuances of expression that deeply influence meaning; missing too are the personality traits that endeared the Rabbi to the faithful audience that sat at his feet regularly during the Sabbath services. Nevertheless, the essence of the message, the appeal not to permit a mood of disenchantment to become a permanent philosophy, emerges clearly. And this evocation is accomplished without artifice. Rabbi Cohon eschewed dramatics; he never relied on flashy phraseology, calculated to substitute shock for reflective attention. His sermons were carefully thought out, stripped of cliché and superficiality, honed to the essential thought that was the spine of his interpretation.

In the long run this method will very likely lend durability to the volume. There is an encouraging renaissance today, especially among our younger people who, in Hanson's words, want to remember the heritage that their fathers, over-eager for quick assimilation, were so anxious to forget. Such a generation will find renewed morale in the author's counsel, even in these most disruptive times: "Come, let us reason together."

Abram L. Sachar

# Preface

MOVING my study into a new apartment, after some thirty years in the previous one, I had occasion to clear an old filing case of accumulated papers, long forgotten. Among these notes — sermon lecture memos, correspondence — I came on a batch of sermons I had laid aside for possible publication at a later date. Reading these old sermons, which had completely faded from my memory, was a sobering experience. Had I really written these, and had I delivered them from the pulpit? Much of the contents sounded far away.

In time, these manuscripts went back to the years 1940, 1941, 1942 — years of violent alarms: Mussolini, Hitler — their bombers and panzer divisions rent the heavens and rocked the earth. They were years of terror. A young Rabbi in his pulpit, facing a modest congregation, mainly personal friends — many seeing their sons going off to war or preparing to be drafted — had fears in his heart. Black clouds of tyranny were gathering everywhere. All the anchors of faith, freedom, democracy, family virtues, religious sanctities, were dragging in the storm. His prayerbook rang hollow. The Jewish world was in rubble. The radios blared the apocalyptic destruction of historic Jewish centers of learning and piety — synagogues, academies turned into stables, refugees jamming the roads and even the high seas without a port to receive them. Our own free America shut its gates to the desperate hordes of men, women and children. What might a Rabbi say to his friends from the pulpit that carried conviction?

I read these dusty old sermons of my earlier years and discarded some, read again and discarded some more. Then came a pause in my haste to discard. We were in dire need of a prophetic word — a word above race, above class, above dogma, above economic determinism, above the despair and cynicism of the day, above the dogmatic pronouncements in the name of science, above psychiatry. Weak and inadequate as these sermons were, the Word had to be spoken, however humbly, however inadequately. The vision must be kept alive, for we know that where there is no vision the people perish. The appeal was to reason and faith in a moral Providence presiding over our human destinies.

A little candle, however modest, betokens a redeeming light. I want to share this little candle with my friends.

A word of thanks to two gracious friends who read these pages and gave me the benefit of their literary talents and kind friendship — Abraham S. Burack and Mrs. Miriam Madfis. Thanks also to my cherished friend, Mrs. Lee Haase, who has been such a comfort to me over the years with her skill as typist and her readiness to cooperate.

Beryl D. Cohon

Brookline, Massachusetts

# COME, LET US REASON TOGETHER

# 1 COME, LET US
REASON TOGETHER

OUR holy days are points of lookout in the realm of
Jewish life. They are observation towers from the
heights of which we may view the land — look down upon
Philistia and survey, also, the Promised Land. They would
lift us from the swampy regions of the ordinary, the me-
diocre, the trivial, and afford us a view of far horizons.
They speak of conscience, duty, destiny, God. Our holy
days should, therefore, deepen insight, clarify the mind
and fortify the will in the realm of the good, the just and
holy. They must stretch the mind and give us deeper understanding, larger sympathies.

In keeping with the high purpose of this holy day (Rosh
Hashanah), I want to focus your attention this morning on
an ideal enunciated by one of our ancient prophets — the
prince of all our prophets, some scholars affirm — Isaiah.
He spoke these words in little Judea some time around
the year 740 before the Christian Era. For over two thousand, six hundred and seventy years his words have served
as a shaft of light, piercing the corridors of these morally
chaotic centuries.

The first chapter of the book of Isaiah may be read as
a prologue to the flaming scroll that holds the prophecies
of Isaiah. Heaven and earth are called upon to serve as
witnesses. God is represented as pleading with His people,

3

pleading with them for their own salvation. "Come now,
let us reason together, saith the Lord. If your sins be as
scarlet, can they become white as snow? If they be red
like crimson, can they become as wool? If ye be willing and
obedient, ye shall eat the good of the land: but if ye refuse
and rebel, ye shall be devoured with the sword, for the
mouth of the Lord hath spoken it."

"Come, let us reason together, says the Lord." Here is
an heroic idea, startling for our own time and especially
for the time when it was first spoken. God *reasons* with
man. He does not proclaim, He does not command, He
does not thunder; He reasons and appeals to human reason. He pleads with man to be rational. And He pleads,
further, that man be just. "If your sins be as scarlet, can
they become white as snow? If they be red like crimson, can
they become as wool?" Of course not. There are moral
cause and effect. Plant iniquity and you reap the whirl-
wind; plant justice and you reap righteousness, stability,
peace.

> The reward of righteousness shall be peace;
> And the effect of righteousness, quietness
> and confidence forever.

The moral law is part of the very structure of the universe.
Violate it and the world feels its shock, and man is doomed.

Man must be reasonable and just. That is the will of
God. Such an interpretation of the Divine Mind is daring.
Other teachers in other religions pleaded with men to
desert the world and retire to a wilderness, far from the
turmoil and conflicts of life, there to find their God. They
have called men to deserts and monasteries and to un-
earthly Nirvanas. They have focused the minds of men on
the hereafter and conditioned them to ignore the immediate world and its pressing injustices and needs. In doing

that, they led men to close their eyes to the evil, the vulgarity and injustice of the world, to be satisfied if they found for themselves choice places among the saints in heaven. This obtained also in Judaism, in part — in the Hasidic, in the cabalistic at times — but this is not the interpretation of the Divine Will given by our prophets. Isaiah, speaking in the name of God, pleads with his countrymen to be reasonable and just. His words have become classic in our faith. Reason and justice — a rational and just humanity in a rational and just world — such is the will of God as understood in prophetic Judaism.

The heroic quality of this thought becomes even more manifest when we recall that Isaiah spoke this doctrine at a time of severe crisis in the life of his nation. Four waves of invasion swept Palestine in the lifetime of Isaiah. The Assyrian legions plundered Judah and reduced to ashes her cities and her cultivated fields, her shrines and her homes. Isaiah knew war, famine, pestilence. Fear and hatred, greed and corruption, disunion in the face of the marauder were enacted before his eyes. He condemned in scathing terms the social evils of his time — arrogance, exploitation of the poor, concentration of wealth, the crowding out of the small farmer, drunkenness, corrupt courts, degenerate priests, bragging skepticism. He branded the popular religion of his people as immoral religion. In the midst of all this mental and moral perversion, he raised his voice in a plea for reason and justice. In reason and justice lay the salvation of the world.

You and I are living at a time when the world is desperately in need of Isaiah's vision of a rational and just humanity in a rational and just world. We pride ourselves on living in an age of science; we flaunt our intellectualism over the superstitions of the Dark Ages. In a measure we are justified. Would that we were completely justified! The stark fact, however, is that though living in an age of science unparalleled in history, though surrounded by uncanny inventions that enable us to soar in the skies, weigh the sun, split the atom, bridge every canyon, explore the bowels of the earth, eradicate diseases that have ravaged mankind since days immemorial, we are, nevertheless, in an age when reason is at bay, when brute force, raw passions and mechanized barbarism are snatching the ground from under us like the undertow of a surging sea, and threaten to sweep us into a new Dark Age. I am not speaking of the appalling moral obtuseness of our civilization — a fearful, ominous theme on which to reflect; I am speaking of one aspect of it — the sheer disdain of reason, the actual fear of reason in large areas of our civilization.

The flight from reason has brought mankind to the verge of catastrophe.* This sad earth of ours has been reduced to a battleground where "ignorant armies clash by night." Reason and freedom have surrendered to brute force, mass mysticism and mob emotionalism, manipulated by dictators and their gangster assistants. God knows how many million men and women have been reduced to robots in the mechanized armies of terror and death! Superstitious racism, class greed, and mad nationalism have blown out the lamps of reason and have left most of humanity to rave and jabber in madness in a dark world.

The first thing dictators do is extinguish the lamps of reason, exploit the fears and passions of men, and regiment their souls. The scholars, the writers, the teachers, the preachers, the scientists, the artists become official liars for the state. Science is reduced to a manipulation of state-controlled dogmas; religion is converted to a worship of Moloch; schools and colleges are reduced to cells for na-

* These words were spoken in the shadow of Hitler and the Holocaust.

tionalistic propaganda; the theater and the concert hall must glorify the state; the press becomes a state bulletin, screaming every lie the dictator commands. The mind is extinguished and the soul is prostituted.

Recently, Harvard University observed its three-hundredth birthday. You and I were thrilled by the spirit of the festivities and by the emphasis upon the free play of the enlightened mind. But we must not allow ourselves to be blinded to the realities of our time. Harvard and the schools it represents — the schools and colleges where the mind is free to investigate, to think, to follow the light — are the exception. They are islands in a sea of superstition, ignorance and arrogance. How long can these islands maintain themselves against the floods of the new barbarism?

Contrast the celebration at Harvard with a celebration held in Germany recently, and you will see dramatized the intellectual and moral crisis of our time.

A month or two ago, Heidelberg University celebrated the five-hundred-fiftieth anniversary of its founding. It is one of the oldest, and, up to the time of its degradation with the rise of the Third Reich, was one of the greatest universities in the world. Scores and scores of its distinguished sons have bestowed rich blessings upon mankind. Over the portal of one of its buildings were inscribed the words, "To the Living Spirit." Last July the inscription was removed. In its place have been cut the words, "To the German Spirit." The real meaning of this change was expressed by one of the official spokesmen for the once-great university. Said this prostituted professor of philosophy, speaking to scholars assembled from all parts of the world: "We do not know of or recognize truth for truth's sake or science for science's sake." The education minister announced before the same distinguished body that Germany has freed herself "from the false idea of objectivity . . . .

Science based on the sovereign right of abstract intellectual activity has gone forever." For giving this direction to the intellectual life of the Reich, the chancellor of the university was promoted. He was raised from lieutenant to captain! This is the same university that at one time had invited Spinoza to its faculty.

Contrast this with the Harvard tercentenary celebration. Speaking before the assembled scholars and alumni, President Conant said:

> A wave of anti-intellectualism is passing round the world. We see evidences of it on every land, but it is no new phenomenon.
>
> For the development of a national culture based on a study of the past, one condition is essential. This is absolute freedom of discussion, absolutely unmolested inquiry. We must have a spirit of tolerance which allows the expression of all opinions however heretical they may appear.

And again:

> If we attempt to sum up in one phrase the aim of higher education we can do no better than to speak of the search for the truth.

Between Heidelberg and Harvard, and the schools that line up behind them, lies the fate of our civilization. It is the ancient conflict between the book and the sword.

The news dispatches from Spain have been reporting the horrible siege of the Alcazar. In that infernal fort thrives a race of blind mice, we are told. They have lived and bred so long in those dark caverns that they have lost their vision. The dictators of the world, with their lying propaganda, their control of schools, pulpits, press, theaters are reducing our world to an Alcazar, and mankind to a race of blind mice.

We cannot renounce reason without renouncing justice.

If we cease being rational, we cease being just. That is
inevitable. If we deny reason its legitimate place in the
life of man, we deny all rational values. We then blot out
such eternal ideals as goodness, beauty, mercy, truth, and,
particularly, justice. The day after Germany outlawed objectivity in jurisprudence came a wireless report, dated
July third, 1936:

> The formal announcement to the world in Heidelberg
> early this week that German science must be National So-
> cialist Science and not a search for 'truth for truth's sake' is
> producing practical results already.
>
> Dr. Wilhelm Coblitz, chief of the Nazi party's bureau for
> control of legal literature, issued in the Ministry of Justice's
> official organ a warning to all authors dealing with juris-
> prudence. He states:
>
> "The Nazi State demands in literature dealing with ju-
> risprudence and law a frank confession of faith in its fun-
> damental political conception.
>
> "The period is over when a science of jurisprudence in-
> dependent of political faith is possible. Jurisprudence
> devoid of a tendency has become impossible. Neutrality in
> regard to the principles of our racial unity will not be
> tolerated.
>
> "The new State will prevent any weakening or misrepre-
> sentation of Nazi ideas regarding justice and the State."

In other words, the scales of justice must not be held
evenly when one of two litigants is not a Nazi. Compare
this with the law proclaimed in Israel more than three
thousand years ago: "One law shall be to him that is home-
born, and unto the stranger that sojourneth among you."

The same principle functions in our personal lives. It is
lack of understanding, lack of insight, lack of appreciation
of the problems and strains under which other people live
that is mostly responsible for man's inhumanity to man.

Most of us offend and hurt not because we are malicious, but because we do not understand. If we are beginning to deal more justly and more humanely with the criminal, the pervert, the demented and erring, it is because modern biology and psychology have opened our eyes to the forces at work in the lives of these unfortunates.

We Jews are heirs to a tradition that has extolled the intellect. We have been the intellectual aristocrats of the world. The divine summons voiced by Isaiah many, many centuries ago became a driving power in Jewish life. "Come, let us reason together." Back in the black depths of the Dark Ages our teachers extolled reason as the link between God and man. Eight hundred years ago Maimonides pleaded for "the intellectual love of God." About the same time Abraham ibn Ezras spoke of reason as "the mediating angel between man and his God." The Psalmist's prayer was ever on the lips of our fathers: "Grant me understanding that I may live."

And by the intellect the Jew has not meant mere intellectual gymnastics, mere nimble logic. The word *sechel* means moral conscience as well as intellect. The wise man has been the good man, the just man, the man of mercy and peace.

Living at a time when there is a flight from reason, when the intellect is derided and feared in wide areas of the world, literally, for the salvation of our own souls, and literally for the salvation of a despairing world, we must keep alive in our own lives and in the lives of our communities our ancient Jewish ideal of intellectual excellence and moral uprightness. The fate of the world hangs on that. Your fate and mine as cultured men and women hang on that.

"Come, let us reason together." Come, let us reason together and be just. An ancient Jewish writer has expressed accurately the true Jewish ideal of the harmony of heart and mind in the search for the good life: "When God made man, He implanted in him His affections and dispositions; and then over all He enthroned the sacred ruling mind." *The sacred ruling mind!*

For many generations our fathers recited this prayer daily. We pray it be realized in our life, in the life of Israel and the life of mankind:

"Thou favorest man with knowledge, and teachest mortals understanding.

O favor us with knowledge, understanding, and discernment from Thee.

Blessed art Thou, O Lord, gracious Giver of knowledge."

# 2 OLD ZEPHENIAH TODAY

ONE of our ancient masters, the prophet Zepheniah —
more than two thousand five hundred years ago —
dreamed of a time when mankind would speak a purer,
nobler language, and Israel would be a redeeming force
in the world. This dream has become part of our Jewish
heritage. This dream we must not lose. "For then will I
turn to the peoples a pure language." The arrogant, the
cruel, the vulgar will no longer be heard in Israel. "The
remnant of Israel shall not do iniquity, nor speak lies,
neither shall a deceitful tongue be found in their mouths."

From the miseries of his day, and from the prophet's
great heart, issued this hope. Surely, this is our hope;
surely, in a purer, nobler speech on the part of all mankind, and especially within our own Jewish household, lies
our salvation. How may we, who share this prophetic hope,
contribute our honest share toward its realization?

*First,* by being more skeptical — skeptical not only of
those with whom we disagree, but skeptical of those with
whom we do agree, skeptical of ourselves and of the words
we ourselves use. It is not easy to be skeptical of ourselves.
We are not real skeptics unless we question our own beliefs and opinions. Smug self-righteousness is the hallmark
of the bigot. Speaking as I do from a synagogue pulpit that

champions faith, I urge skepticism. Skepticism is imperative today to keep the lamps of faith burning. Today, skepticism is an essential of the moral life. There are too many
propagandists loose in the world; too many spiritual
quacks; too many men with glib tongues and addled minds;
too many lying presses, lying television sets, lying radios,
lying forums, lying pulpits. Too many charlatans are in-
terpreting the word of God. We must develop the skepticism that demands facts and logic and basic, rugged personal integrity, or we shall be stampeded by these eloquent
liars. It is easier to listen and applaud, to read and approve,
than to think and, if need be, dissent. We should take a
page out of the autobiography of George Herbert Palmer:
"On leaving college," he wrote, "I had absorbed more than
I had digested and I resolved to take a year of comparative
leisure for reviewing and thinking of what I had read."

A *second* thing we must do if we are to escape the shib-
boleth-mouthing mobs, and that is to find a retreat from
the din and clatter of our noisy world. We must step aside
for a time to gain perspective. Many have urged that we
go to the mountains occasionally, and in the silence, majesty and awesome patience of these formations find our
souls. Some of us are wise enough, and fortunate enough,
to find a retreat, and to find ourselves, in some sequestered
corner away from the highways. Some find a retreat in
good books and noble music. All of us can have that if
we will it.

I covet for the Synagogue the function of a retreat, redeeming the Jewish masses from the fierce strife of slogans
and selling gimmicks. The Synagogue should be beyond
partisanship, beyond impassioned arrogance, beyond pan-
dering to the vulgarized tastes of people. It has the power
to be that if it would only be true to itself as the reposi-
tory of Israel's heritage. The idealism of our prophets,

sages, psalmists, poets, rabbis, martyrs is our heritage. "All ye who are thirsty come ye to the waters, drink and let your souls live," Isaiah speaks to us across the ages. Thus has the Synagogue sustained our fathers and made of them an invincible people. Israel has weathered every storm and has risen above every despair by the faith and fortitude and stubborn integrity cultivated in the Synagogue. Today it is the only institution we have that gives meaning to our life as a distinctive group and moral warrant to our separateness. If we remain true to the Synagogue, and insist that it, in turn, be true to itself as the central shrine of world Jewry, as the guardian and protagonist of all that is sacred, we shall thereby do our share as a Jewish group to help make the accents of a purer, nobler speech heard in a sick world.

# 3 | FREE MEN OR ROBOTS?

ONE of the most precious aspects of our Jewish moral heritage is the high value placed upon the individual as a free, morally-responsible agent. Our masters emphasized the "sanctity of personality." That is an imperative lesson for us to continue and advance. You and I as Jews cannot give the world anything it needs more desperately in this troubled day than a renewed respect for the individual and emphasis upon his rights and his duties. I am stressing this because we are living at a time when the individual is crushed. Evil philosophies are rampant in the world. One pernicious doctrine they have in common, and that is reducing the individual to a mere tool in the power of the state. Be it Fascism or Communism, the individual is so regimented that he loses his own identity; he ceases being a responsible person and becomes a robot. That is the most immoral thing that is happening in our time.

Reflect upon these words of our masters.

Ben Azai, a Talmudic sage who taught some eighteen hundred years ago, found the key to the entire Torah and the central lesson of Judaism in the Biblical sentence: "This is the book of the generations of man. In the day that God created man, in the likeness of God made He him." Man is made in the "image of God"; he holds within

himself a breath of the divine. His life is, therefore, sacred.
It is inviolable. Only God gives life; only God may take it.
The Talmudic masters thus emphasize that he who destroys a single human being is as one who destroys a
whole world. You remember the story of Abraham pleading with God to save a wicked city for the sake of the
ten upright men who may be among its inhabitants. And
the Righteous Judge of all the earth agreed to spare a city
of evil-doers should there be ten innocent men within her
gates. "That be far from Thee to do after this manner, to
slay the righteous with the wicked . . . that be far from
Thee. Shall not the Judge of all the earth do justly?"

Man is a co-worker with God himself. The Holy One
cannot build a just world unless man cooperates. The individual finds the meaning of his life, attains his true dignity and realizes his destiny by serving as a co-worker with
the Supreme Master.

The rabbis are careful to point out that though the Law
revealed at Sinai was given to the whole community of Israel, it was commanded to every Jew individually, "according to the power of each" to comprehend. Think what
a truly redeeming concept this is, and please remember
that it was enunciated some eighteen hundred years ago.
Not a social order that reduces all men to a race of stan-
dardized robots, but one that recognizes respectfully the
special capacities and unique endowments of each.

We can have no truth, no justice, and no peace in the
world as long as we do not share fully this high respect
for the sanctity of the individual life and for the inviol-
ability of personality. Whatever social philosophy we may
expound, whatever system of government or economics
we may embrace, we must remember that the source and
the creative power of any social order is the individual. To
build a social order by reducing men and women to a race

of robots is to rear an immoral society which cannot and should not exist. Nearly a century ago, John Stuart Mill wrote these words; they have a special significance for us today:

> The worth of a state in the long run is the worth of the individuals composing it. . . . . a state which dwarfs its men in order that they may be more docile instruments in its hands, even for beneficial purposes, will find that with small men no great thing can really be accomplished.

Fascists and Communists should ponder this statement. Today, we are witnessing an appalling thing: contempt for the individual's rights, liberties, and capacities. Fascism regiments the individual and Communism "liquidates" him. The world over, the individual is prostituted by lying propaganda and race or class hatreds. In this degradation of the individual, the gains of moral civilization perish.

Consider this quotation culled at random from the daily press, and note the moral degradation of our time. The German minister of propaganda is reported by an Associated Press dispatch to have said recently:

> To be a human being is in itself nothing. A flea is also an animal, but that does not make it by any means a pleasant animal.

He was meeting the argument that the Jews, after all, are human beings. Contrast this with the teaching of the rabbis that the human personality is God's highest creation and that it is divine and, hence, inviolable. To be a human being is in itself nothing! He has no rights. The state can be as arbitrary as it pleases. In Jewish tradition God Himself cannot be arbitrary with man. Job would plead his case before God; he reasons and demands an explanation of the Almighty Himself. The Almighty praises him for it. The contemptuous attitude expressed by the German barbarian is typical of the attitudes toward the individual taken by all dictators. That is the basic immorality of dictatorships. And because the individual is held in such contempt, laws are passed and so-called "reforms" are instituted that shock the enlightened mind. Sterilization, it seems, is being applied with brutal callousness. There is a case for and there is a case against sterilization, but the readiness of political gangsters, drunk with power, to apply it is shocking. Marriages are formed and marriages are dissolved very much the way breeding is arranged among animals. Recently, the divorce rate in Russia reached the figure of forty-four to a hundred marriages. The government, alarmed, is taking measures to make marriages more permanent. Germany, Italy, and Russia, especially, are preoccupied with the management of the birth rate. Bonuses, marriage loans, tax exemptions are employed. Why are these nations so greedy for a higher birth rate? They are choked with people as it is; thousands upon thousands cannot find employment; hungry hordes are everywhere. One would think that a higher birth rate would be discouraged. Why seek a larger population? The answer is obvious, of course! They need more soldiers, more cannon fodder, more robots.

Soviet Russia has reduced its contempt for the individual as an individual to a creed. Reliable correspondents report that the Russian famine, which took four million lives some years ago, was avoidable, that the Government deliberately allowed four million men, women, and children to perish—to teach the stubborn peasants a lesson! It has been estimated that between Stalin, Mustapha Kemal, Hitler, and Mussolini, three hundred million people were reduced to serfdom. They are the new helots. By an evil logic and cruel power, three hundred million people, in only four countries of the world, are reduced to political cattle.

What is happening to the sanctity of personality and the rights and liberties of the individual?

The backwash of this immorality is bound to reach our shores. Many claim that our American waters are already polluted with it. It is not within my scope, nor is it within my competence, to discuss the ethics of the so-called New Deal or Old Deal. But issues are involved that transcend party interests or personal preferences. Do you not agree with me that in this morally-chaotic day the most imperative test of all things that we Jews can urge on the world about us is the effects upon the individual person? Will it make the individual stronger, and will it make him more just? Will it make him more self-reliant, more responsible, more fair, more considerate? This is the ultimate test that we must apply. Every conceivable test seems to be applied to our national policies but this one. A balanced budget, the volume of trade, the number of employed or unemployed, higher or lower prices, the number of car loadings, the volume of exports or imports—these are the tests we employ in ascertaining our national well-being. I am not saying that they should not be employed. What I am saying is that beyond all our tests and all our policies, we must view, and view totally, the individual life, and we must be jealous for its rights and its liberties, for its possibilities, and for its responsibilities. If "wealth accumulates and men decay," all our policies and all our improvements as recorded on the charts and in the indexes will be not only ultimate failures but immoral.

I am not pleading for unbridled individualism. A *laissez-faire* society can crush the individual as effectively as can the regimented state. The mob is forever with us to down him who would rise above it. Our herd life and our standardization of all things will keep us close enough to the common denominator. As long as human society is made up of human beings who vary widely in their aptitudes, capacities, and ambitions, the lambs will have to be protected from the wolves. We Jews, who have emphasized the sanctity of individual life and have shown such a profound respect for the individual, have, nevertheless, evolved codes to regulate our social life. We have evolved codes from the Ten Commandments through the Talmud and the Shulkan Aruk. While shielding and cultivating the individual, we have also sought to restrain him and socialize him. But the purpose of government is not to suppress the individual; the purpose of government is to insure the rights and liberties and opportunities of the individual. The state exists for the individual; the individual does not exist for the state. This principle is being reversed today. The supreme Moloch is the state, the Fascist State, or the Communist Soviet, or by whatever name it may be known.

We Jews are the guardians of a precious heritage. Lawgivers, prophets, martyrs have endowed us with the vision of a morally responsible community in a covenant with the Eternal. The ancient prophet speaks to us from the despairs of his own day: "Stand on your feet, son of man, and I will speak to you." Man is born to be free; no man is born to be a chained helot in a brutal state. That is the redeeming vision for us Jews to shield in our stormy day.

The voice of the prophet is haunting:

> Then shall thy light break forth as the morning . . .
> And they that shall be of thee
>     shall build the old waste places,
> Thou shalt raise up the foundations of many
>     generations;
> And thou shalt be called the repairer of the breach,
> The restorer of paths to dwell in.

# 4 THE FATHERS HAVE EATEN SOUR GRAPES

A PROVERB was current in ancient Israel which the prophet Ezekiel quotes and refutes. This proverb and this refutation summarize a much-debated issue in the history of Judaism. Today the proverb still expresses a philosophy of life popular the world over, and the prophet's refutation is still a pointed challenge. As we accept or reject or adapt the formula given by our priest-prophet in the dim days of the Babylonian exile, more than two thousand five hundred years ago, so shall we determine the moral content of our civilization. Thus shall we determine, too, whether we shall live and prosper as a race of men, or rear a generation of spineless creatures, breeding a race of opportunists.

> And the word of the Lord came unto me, saying: What mean ye that ye use this proverb in the land of Israel, saying:
> The fathers have eaten sour grapes,
> And the children's teeth are set on edge?
> As I live saith the Lord God, ye shall not have occasion any more to use this proverb in Israel. Behold, all souls are Mine; as the soul of the father, so also the soul of the son is Mine; the soul that sinneth, it shall die.

The proverb seems to have been popular with the He-

brew masses. A decade or two before Ezekiel, the prophet
Jeremiah had quoted it and expressed his fervent hope that
better, happier days were coming and that in those days the
proverb would no longer be heard in the land. It was but
natural for our remote ancestors by the rivers of Babylon
to slip into the type of thinking reflected in this proverb.
They were exiles in a strange land; their country was pros-
trate under the heels of the invader; their dear ones were
murdered; their homes and their national shrine were in
ashes. God had deserted them, they felt. The stern voices
of their earlier prophets were ringing in their ears, rousing
a sense of guilt. They were being punished for their national sins. Their fathers had eaten sour grapes; now they,
the children, were having aching teeth.

The proverb fell from the lips of the Hebrew masses
freighted with despair and cynicism. "We are lost, a
doomed generation; we are helpless and hopeless," many of
them said. We are caught like fish in a net. There is nothing that the individual can do about it. God is angry and
He has rejected us. Another group said, "There are no justice and no truth in the scheme of things. No just God
presides over our destinies. One generation eats sour
grapes and another pays for it. Where is justice? Where is
equity? Where is truth?" Like Job, they challenged God's
justice. "The world is given over into the power of the
wicked. If not He, who?" Still others found themselves confused and bewildered, unable to follow the logic that
pointed to an unjust, capricious Sovereign presiding over
the destinies of men and nations, dooming the innocent
and the guilty alike. These people, again like Job, searched
their hearts, felt themselves innocent of personal guilt, and
pleaded for an explanation. The heavens held no revela-
tion for them.

The proverb still appeals to the minds of the masses. It

has a special appeal today. Men are repeating it every-where, though in different words. The social reformer says: It is environment and heredity that determine the paths we take through life; environment and heredity, not our own wills, shape our destinies. The sociologist, the political reformer, says it is the system under which we live that is responsible for our ills. There is no sense quarreling with the individual, who is helplessly enmeshed. Change the system, pass new laws, reorganize the economic and po-litical setup if you are seeking a happier world. The biol-ogist says it is all in the protoplasm, in the genes. Our ancestors have determined what we are and what we are to be. The psychologist says the deep, mysterious recesses of the subconscious, the inhibitions of our childhood, the primitive impulses determine our personalities and our worth. The alienist in court pleads, not guilty! Why punish the criminal? He is mentally and emotionally miscon-ceived. He is a patient and should be treated as a patient. If we must punish anybody, we should punish his parents and grandparents for transmitting a bad heritage; punish society for not surrounding him with the proper influences. In endless novels, essays, biographies, plays, orations, ser-mons, the erring are absolved of all responsibility.

Thus is the proverb, condemned by the prophet centu-ries upon centuries ago, popular today. It is our fathers' feast of sour grapes that is to blame for all the evil in our own personal conduct.

We Jews have an added bunch of sour grapes to explain away our personal shortcomings. Anti-Semitism is a con-venient cloak. Are we failures in our business enterprises, in our professions? Are we excluded from this or that so-cial set? Are we blackballed in this or that lodge or club? Are our sons and daughters excluded from certain schools? Are we not wanted in certain neighborhoods? Are we gen-

erally disliked? Anti-Semitism is the ready explanation.
Anti-Semitism is the balm of Gilead to some of us when
we are face to face with failure.

Of course, anti-Semitism explains some of it. Many fine
Jewish young men and women are not admitted to certain
schools for no other reason than that the Jewish quotas are
filled. Many of us are not wanted as neighbors for no other
reason than that we are Jews. Many of us in the professions cannot attract a certain clientele for no better reason
than social anti-Semitism. That is true enough. At the same
time, the truth ought to be driven home that it is an evil,
a corrupting thing to cover up our personal shortcomings
with the blind label "anti-Semitism." Are there no misfits
among us? Do we not have our human share of incompe-
tents? It is not true that every time a Jewish boy is excluded
from a college the explanation is anti-Jewish prejudice. He
may have a poor scholastic record or an objectionable personality. It is not true that every time a Jewish family is
excluded from an apartment building or a certain neigh-
borhood the explanation is always hatred of Jews. The
family may be objectionable because of bad social habits.
It is not true that the reason that some of our doctors or
lawyers or businessmen do not prosper is anti-Semitism.
Anti-Semitism may be the reason in part, but not always.
Personal incompetence, lack of integrity or skill, a difficult
personality, or a complicated set of factors which have nothing at all to do with anti-Semitism may explain it. It is a
bad habit we have acquired of condoning every personal
failure on the basis of anti-Semitism. Moreover, as long as
we jump to the hasty and comforting conclusion of anti-
Semitism, we shall never correct our own faults.

I grant that there is truth, much vital truth, in the claims
of the biologist and psychologist, sociologist and economist.
I grant that Ezekiel is woefully antedated in his under-

standing of the roles heredity and environment play in the shaping of our characters and our destinies. I agree with those who say that our political and economic setup must be revised at many points if we are to solve the chronic economic and moral problems of the individual. However, somewhere in our economic, political, and social reforms, somewhere in our educational system, somewhere in our religious teaching and preaching, we must find room for personal responsibility. A theory of life or social reform that ignores personal responsibility is fatal. "The soul that sinneth, *it* shall die." It, and none other. We must not exonerate the individual too easily. At every point in our lives — in our personal conduct as parents or as children, as friends, as neighbors, as workers, whatever our vocations, whatever our problems, whatever the temptations that beset us, whatever our heredities and our environments — personal responsibility for what we are and do, and what we try to be and to do, must not be explained away too readily. I cannot conceive any moral, ethical religion without a strong emphasis on personal responsibility. "The soul that sinneth, *it* shall die." I plead for "rugged individualism" in the realm of moral integrity. I plead for the ancient, orthodox virtue of recognizing one's personal responsibilities and discharging one's honest personal duties.

The habit of exonerating the individual of all personal responsibility leads, inevitably, to futility. I need not point out what effects the constant plea of "not guilty," "not responsible" must have upon character. What type of individual may we envisage under such influence?

But more than that: having freed the individual of all responsibility, we go about solving our problems impersonally. That leads to vicarious virtues or to a mimeographed idealism. We vote for this or that candidate, and that is the measure of our personal contribution to the so-

lution of the stupendous problems that beset us. We sign a
resolution calling for disarmament, and that is our contribution to the cause of world peace. We give the solicitor
a dollar or two, and that settles our own personal responsibility to the misery of our community.

I want to suggest several areas where a larger measure of
personal responsibility must be achieved. With our present
tendency to concentrate power and effort in national offices,
with the expansion of business enterprises and the tendency to deal more and more impersonally in our social
thought and service, the slump in personal responsibility
becomes an acute problem.

*First* is our way of thinking. We must clear the mind of
certain shibboleths and get rid of bad mental habits if we
are to understand properly the moral issues plaguing our
generation.

We speak of "society" and "system." Many among us feel
that once we have recreated our society and reorganized
our economic or political system, our problems will be
solved and Utopia will be around the corner. That is part
of the avalanche of balderdash that is overwhelming us. Of
course, we must revise our social and economic order. I am
not defending blindly the present scheme of things in every
detail. But, after all, any society rests on individual men
and women. Imperative as social organization may be, individual regeneration must accompany our reforms, or we
shall be exchanging one woe for another, one form of cru-
elty for another. You cannot build an enduring structure
with rotten material; you cannot build a better world with
rotten men and women.

There is a small group, for instance, seeking to cure all
our Jewish ills by reorganizing the Jewish community.
"Reconstruct Judaism," we are told. "Reorganize it into a
civilization. Reconstruct our social welfare setup; reorga-

nize our schools." There is a great deal in Jewish life that needs reconstruction; that is a matter of efficiency. But if we wish to bring more health, more vigor into Jewish life, more loyalty to high ideals, we must concern ourselves not so much with the reorganization of the community as with the regeneration of the individual Jew.

We pass resolutions interminably. There is something ridiculous about most of our resolutions. They reveal a jejune state of mind. We cannot solve pressing, complicated problems with resolutions. That is paper idealism.

We enact laws. Of course, in this complicated age, new situations are forever arising that require new safeguards. But it is a futile thing to enact legislation when what we need is education. Have we not learned anything from the Prohibition fiasco? Will we never learn that we cannot legislate people into righteousness, into idealism, into virtue?

The story is told of a certain farmer who wrote to his Senator urging him to vote for a certain pure-food law then before the legislature. The Senator knew that farmer and was surprised at the communication. The man was known to adulterate the syrup he was marketing. The proposed law would go hard on him. The Senator wrote to him accordingly. The farmer replied: "Yes, I am accused of adding brown sugar to the syrup; that is why I want you to vote for that law. I want you to pass a law to stop me from doing it."

A *second* area where individual responsibility must be restored is our business world. The corporate form of business does away with personal responsibility. When the business world was simpler and a man dealt with his customers directly, there was a good measure of personal honor involved. One's good name was at stake; one's family tradition had to be maintained. One took pride in his word. His humanity was alive and responsive. But all this is deadened in the corporate form of business dealing. Men do things in the name of corporations which they dare not do in their own names.

I am not advocating the abandonment of the corporate form of business, but I am pleading that a full measure of personal responsibility be restored. How that is to be achieved, I do not know; that is the problem before the enlightened businessman, the businessman who is something more than a mere shrewd exploiter. The teacher of Judaism can only commend to the conscience, hoping that there is enough conscience to which to appeal. The teacher of Judaism, moreover, has enough faith in the goodness and honor of the average person to feel that his is not futile talk when he speaks to the aroused conscience of decent men.

A *third* area where individual responsibility is sorely lacking and where it must be created is journalism. Our anonymous journalism is a moral evil of first magnitude. Why shall not the editor and the writer assume full responsibility for their writings? They are molding public opinion; they speak for the nation; they are behind or against everything that is good or evil. Their influence is thus enormous. Why may we not hold them accountable for the views they foster and the policies they encourage? If businessmen take refuge in the corporate form of business and engage in piracy, journalists hide behind a double screen — the enormous corporations of their publications and, further, behind anonymity and editorial policy. We read newspapers every day of our lives. Do we know who edits our newspaper — who writes its editorials? Men should sign their names to whatever they write and assume full praise or blame for the veracity of their data.

We are impatient with men when we find them insincere. We are severe on the preacher when he proves himself hypocritical. Why condone blatant insincerity in the realm of the written word?

A *fourth* area is religion. Personal integrity is the very essence of religion. Impersonal religion is a contradiction in terms. The religious person is impelled and directed in thought and behavior by a sense of the sacred. Religion speaks to the individual in terms of individual duty. "And the word of the Lord came unto *me*," is a recurrent phrase in the Bible; not "to humanity" but to "me." Enlightened religion has a social message, of course, but the social ideals require personal dedication or they are pretense and sham.

One of the weaknesses of organized religion is that it has fallen victim to size. "The curse of bigness" is upon it. It has become another corporation. It is concerned too much with numbers. The quality of teaching and preaching has become impersonal. I am afraid that degeneration is rapidly eating at the very heart of our synagogues. We fulminate too much on anti-Semitism; we beat the wind too much with economic, political, literary abstractions. We do not drive into the hearts and minds of our men and women the divine compulsion of "Thus saith the Lord." We are not concerned enough with the personal problems, personal needs of the men and women who compose our congregations.

Judaism has always thought in terms of individual responsibility. Its message of social justice has drawn the admiration of the thinking world; but it is its insistence upon individual duty and personal integrity that has given reality to its social pronouncements.

In conclusion, I address an added word to a special number among you within the hearing of my voice. Some of you are people of considerable influence. Wealth, social prestige, family traditions, ability, culture have lifted you into positions of influence. A special responsibility, therefore, rests upon you. You set the pace. You, therefore, help ennoble Jewish life or help vulgarize it. Your attitude toward Jewish ideals, the measure of responsibility you personally assume toward Synagogue and school, the contribution that you make — financially and spiritually — determine the attitudes many are to take. A grave responsibility, therefore, rests upon you. If you are seen in the house of your God, others will follow; if your children are seen in our Jewish schools, others will send their children; if you shoulder your honest duties, others will act honorably; but if you sneer and shirk and offer subtle excuses, you will thereby lead others to do the same. Will you not give this fact your full, honest consideration and make peace with your God in the privacy of your own hearts? God be with you and guide you.

# 5 | BUILDING A SANCTUARY AND DESTROYING IT

FOR the past several weeks we have been reading portions of the Torah that deal with the building of the ancient sanctuary by our remote ancestors as they sought their way through the wilderness to the Promised Land. We shall continue reading references to this theme in the weeks before us. The story is confused in places; it is fragmentary in spots; it is made up of many patches of tradition. Certain controlling ideas, however, are clear. In the matter of the building of the tabernacle and the later sanctuary — as told in these chapters in the Pentateuch and in the prophetic supplements — at least three principles should be noted. Appreciation of them will help us understand our own heritage better; more than that, it will help us gain mature insight into the life of the spirit today.

First, the people called to build the sanctuary must be fit and equal to the sacred task. Not everybody is called. Only "the wise hearted" are summoned — the wise hearted; the *hachman lev*. They that have the necessary nobility of soul are the ones who are entrusted with the sacred task. According to the notions of our Biblical ancestors, the heart was the seat of intelligence, not the brain, as we think today. And when they spoke of *hochma*, wisdom, they meant not only the heart but also the head.

Elsewhere in the Bible is the injunction, "Ye shall be whole-hearted with the Lord your God." By that they meant, as the rabbis pointed out, whole, complete, worshipping God with all our personalities — not emotion only, not intellect only, not aesthetics only, not stern morals only; we must worship God with our complete personalities, with all the good faculties with which God has endowed us.

The *first* principle, then, in the building of a sanctuary is that it must be built by people who are spiritually-minded, who are decently disposed, who have the necessary nobility of heart and quality of mind.

The *second* principle is that the material used must be perfect; the material of which the shrine is built, the offerings placed upon it, must be without blemish. The leading artist of the time, Bezalel, is summoned to the task. The gold, the silver, the crystals, the linen, the oil must be perfect. The rabbis carried this principle into later Judaism. The *etrog* must not have any blemish, however, slight; the *sukkah* must be beautiful. The Sabbath and the festivals must be artistically observed. The materials and the offerings must be aesthetically fit. The diseased, the sickly, the crippled animal must not be given to the sanctuary. It is the first fruits, the excellent, that must be devoted to the altar. The hire of a harlot must not be devoted to the sanctuary. The materials and the offerings must be *voluntarily* given. There must be no resentment or reluctance of spirit associated with the building of a sanctuary. "Take ye from among you an offering unto the Lord, whosoever is of a willing heart, let him bring it. . . . And they came, every one whose heart stirred him up, and every one whose heart made him willing, and brought the Lord's offering." Artistically, aesthetically perfect, voluntarily, gladly given — that is required. Good intentions are not enough; pious sentiment is not enough; giving from our superfluity is not enough; the offerings must be tangible, real, representing a personal sacrifice.

The *third* principle controlling the building of the tabernacle to which I wish to call your attention is the ultimate purpose of the tabernacle. Why are tabernacles built? Why are temples erected? They are not for God but for man; God does not need our temples and our churches and our mosques; God does not need our prayers, our hymns, our sermons; but humans need them. A Biblical verse puts it neatly: "Ye shall build me a sanctuary that I may dwell among them." Why "among them"? Should not the sentence read, grammatically, "Build me a sanctuary that I may dwell in it"? The rabbis emphasize that the verse means to say: "Build me a sanctuary that I may dwell among *them*" — in the lives of those who build it. Sanctuaries are built that God may dwell in the hearts of men.

This, then, is the way sanctuaries are built; the workers must be noble-minded people, the material must be aesthetically, morally perfect; the impelling vision must be there — the vision that transforms a stone into an altar. Negate these and you have the deadliest formula for the destruction of our sanctuaries.

You and I often speak with apprehension of the future of the Synagogue. We certainly hear words of warning and alarm. The Philistines are upon us, we are told; the anti-Semite is loose in the world, trampling down all that is sacred to us; our young are not with us; our middle-aged are largely indifferent; even our aged folk are pampered, spiritually exhausted and lazy. There is, of course, much truth in this. I do not mean to deny it. But what I do want to emphasize is this aspect of our problem. Ultimately, synagogues are not destroyed from the outside; synagogues are destroyed from the inside. The anti-Semites can and do demolish our synagogue buildings; they can and do cripple our sons and daughters and scatter them as refugees. But anti-Semites cannot destroy our sanctuaries. We Jews destroy our sanctuaries. And it is not the unaffiliated Jews who destroy our synagogues. They have simply deserted their posts. We have always had unaffiliated folk. They are not the ones who ultimately destroy our temples and disrupt our congregations. The people on the inside do that, and they do that quite unconsciously. They do that by bringing into our congregational life not the nobility of heart that is required, but something else — an alien heart. It may be an ambitious heart — personally ambitious for worldly advancement, utilizing the altar as a stepping-stone; it may be a narrow, hard, irreligious heart; it may be a vulgar, spiritually irresponsive heart. The offerings may be unworthy — tainted, unlovely, dishonest, given grudgingly, given resentfully.

A colleague, whom I hold in esteem, was complaining to me some time ago about the state of the synagogues of New York City. It was not the mortgages or the comparatively few people at services that were worrying him; it was the shabby leadership that distressed him. Most synagogues were political cells, he complained; they are bandwagons for ambitious men to climb into public office. How accurate a statement it is, I do not know; but I think that all of us are mature enough and worldly enough to know that there is much truth in what he said — entirely too much!

I assure you that I value attendance at services; I assure you I place a great deal of value upon our synagogue programs. But of what good are large crowds, and of what good are our programs of activities, if the vision for which the temple stands is not alive? Better, far better, to have a small religious congregation within our temple walls than to have a large crowd that has no sympathy, no appreciation for the truly religious. Our fathers were wise when they stipulated that we need only ten men to constitute a *min-yan* — not a hundred, not even twenty-five, but ten — ten righteous religious men come to pray.

We who are devoted to the religious values in life, and particularly in Jewish life, should make peace with the fact that we are in a minority, that we must work with a minority. But if we of the minority are noble-hearted about it, if we bring the excellence of our spirit and keep before us the vision of the sacred, we shall live and triumph, and our work will endure.

Sanctuaries are built not for God but for the people who build them. You and I kindle and tend the fires upon the altars not because God needs them but because we need God. In the private recesses of our hearts we carry our own sanctuaries. Blessed of the Lord are we if we are so endowed. God grant you and me the wisdom, the capacity and the skill to keep the fires upon these altars burning, and our lives radiated and cheered.

# 6 | DOES JOB SERVE GOD FOR NAUGHT?

IT was the Satan, as reported in the book of Job, who asked one of the most searching questions that disturbs the religious life. The Satan questions Job's motives — and ours. "Does Job serve God for naught?" he asks. We can almost see the devil wag his tail, grin and wink as he fires his question. What frightened faces, open mouths, and nervous flapping of wings there must have been among the angels! "Does Job serve God for naught?" His own answer is: Of course not! It pays to be good; therefore Job is good. "Have you not made a hedge about him, and about his house, and about all that he has on every side? You have blessed the work of his hands, and his possessions are increased in the land. But put forth your hand now and touch all that he has; surely, he will blaspheme you to your face." That is, Job's piety is nothing but a shrewd bargain. It's a "good buy."

Is that a fair answer? Are we religious, to whatever extent we are, because it pays to be? Please remember that the Satan referred not only to Job's formal religiosity and not only to his beliefs; he referred to Job's complete integrity. Job was an upright man, one who shunned evil in every form. One of the loftiest descriptions of the ideal man is given of Job. He was father to the fatherless, pro-

36

tector and provider to the helpless, kind master to his servants, wise counselor to the weary and heavy-laden; lust, greed, selfishness were transmuted in his personality into generosity, kindliness, and self-sacrifice.

> I was eyes to the blind,
> And feet was I to the lame.
> I was a father to the needy;
> And the cause of him that I knew not I searched out.

The rich and the poor, the lowly and the great alike blessed him. All this was part of his religion, and all this, says the Satan, was only a shrewd bargain the sagacious Job was driving with his God. Is the Satan right?

The Satan was never popular. As he evolved into the devil of popular mythology, he became a disreputable character. The religious masters in Christendom, even more than in Jewry, heaped upon him their pious scorn; they attributed to him every evil of the world they could not explain in view of a just, loving God presumed to be presiding over our destinies. In time he became the very source and symbol of all that is cruel, bitter, vicious in human life. They, therefore, recoiled from every sentiment that came in his name. They repudiated scornfully his assertion that Job was calculating in his piety. In the end, Job is vindicated; the Satan is refuted.

But the question still stands. It cannot be dismissed with mere righteous indignation. It is valid. It is pointed. One need not be a Satan to raise it.

Many of the rewards sought by supposedly religious people are foolish. They reveal a childish, even a primitive, view of religion. Recently, our local newspapers reported that a certain woman, here in our own city, found herself on railroad tracks facing an approaching train. Instead of jumping out of the way as best she might, she dropped to her knees in prayer, asking God to save her. Many a person reading of her instant death must have pointed to the news item and said, "That shows you what prayer is good for!" Many mature people, people who have lived long and experienced much, when confronted by religious issues, think like pampered children. They would bargain with God. They would be the favorites of the Almighty. They speak a prayer and expect, in return, long life, immunity from pain, worldly prosperity here below, eternal bliss in the Great Beyond. They expect the laws of nature to be suspended in their favor. Why should illness ever come upon them? Why should death ever intrude into their family circles? Why should old age come upon them? In all the vast universe, in all time and in all space, they would be exceptions. And they fret and fuss, nurse a grudge against God and man, make themselves miserable and bring misery into the lives of those about them when the normal and the inevitable experiences of life come to them.

What are the great gifts that you and I, as reasonably cultivated and reasonably rational men and women, may legitimately seek in the courts of our God? What may we ask religion to give us? Let us look into the lives of the great religious personalities and see what unique characteristics lifted them above the crowd. Thus will we note what religion did for them.

One characteristic that distinguishes the religious geniuses is something that might be described as a sense of divine guidance. The immediacy of God motivates their thought, their feeling, their conduct. They are possessed by an overpowering force; they are drawn to it as the moth is drawn to the light, as the needle is drawn to the magnet. In contact with the Supreme Power they find no peace unless they obey His will. They become instruments, at times unwilling instruments, by means of which God and His

purposes are revealed to them. A few examples from the
lives of religious heroes will help make this clear.

The recurrent sentence in the utterance of the Hebrew
prophets is "Thus saith the Lord." It is not the prophet
but God who is speaking. The prophet is the mouthpiece.
The hand of God is upon him; he can not throw off the
call. The prophet Amos, asked why he persisted in his trea-
sonable speech, answered:

> The lion hath roared, who shall not fear?
> The Lord God hath spoken, who shall not prophesy?

Once the roar of the lion strikes our eardrums, our whole
beings tremble; once the voice of God strikes our souls, our
whole personalities become vibrant with His presence. The
prophet Isaiah feels himself as a man set apart from his
fellows, a lonely, solitary figure, because God has touched
his lips and transformed him. Perhaps the most touching
expression of this is made by Jeremiah. He was haunted by
the immediacy of God. One of the most sensitive passages
in the Bible is a confession by Jeremiah:

> Thou hast seized me, O Lord, and hast enthralled me;
> Thou has laid Thine hand upon me and hast
>     overpowered me.
> If I say, "I will not make mention of Him,
> Nor speak any more in His name,"
> Then there is in my heart as it were a burning fire
> Shut up in my bones,
> And I weary myself to hold it in
> But cannot.

The religious geniuses were possessed by the Eternal;
they could not evade Him.

Socrates — not a Hebrew prophet and not a Christian
saint but a "pagan" — felt himself possessed by "the God
within me," as he put it. If he went about teaching and de-
bating and arguing and, finally, surrendering his life in

consequence, it was because he could not betray his God. His words to the Athenian jury ring with the divine compulsion that characterizes all religious geniuses in Judaism and in Christianity:

> Men of Athens, I honor and love you, but I shall obey God rather than you . . . For I know that this is the command of God, and I believe that no greater good has ever happened in the state than my service to the God . . . . Wherefore, O men of Athens, I say to you, do as Anytus bids or not as Anytus bids, and either acquit me or not; but whichever you do, understand that I shall never alter my ways, not even if I have to die many times.

You and I as ordinary men and women, walking in the beaten paths of conventional life, do not feel the hand of God upon ourselves. His voice may be barely audible, or, we may think, entirely mute; and when we do hear it, we are told that we ought to go to a psychiatrist and have it silenced. But we do speak of conscience; we do profess to a sense of right; we do know that there is a lash at the back of every great thinker. We would not betray a trust; we would not defame a friend; we would not steal or kill; we do defend certain areas in our lives as holy and would surrender our lives, even as Socrates did, rather than allow their defilement; we do thrill to beauty; we do respond to greatness; we do have capacities for self-sacrifice. To religious minds these capacities and these impulses are the broken rays of God transfiguring brute into man. That is the divine compulsion in you and in me. That is one gift we not only have the *right* to seek in our sanctuaries — that is one benefit we *must* seek. If we do not, our religion has no reality.

The sense of a divine Presence endows the religiously sensitive with moral power. That is a *second* benefit we derive from true, genuine religion. Religious people are fearless and original in evaluating all things. Truly religious people do not imitate; they do not act the sedulous ape. Truly religious men and women are not opportunists. They do not follow the crowd. They are rather lonely in the crowd. They do not scramble for the same prizes of the world as do the people about them. What the world calls good they may find repulsive; what the world finds sweet they may find distasteful. And they have the courage to follow their visions. They are original, and they are fearless in the realm of moral values.

Recall a number of examples from our history.

Abraham is the father of our faith. He is the first protagonist of the one God. Once possessed by the vision of the one "God of all the earth" — a daring, original concept which gave him a new world view — he deserts the beaten paths, forsakes his own parents and his native land, and strikes out into an unknown world, guided by the light within him. The sentence in the Bible describing this adventure is symbolic of all religious geniuses, though they may have remained close to their homes all their lives: "Now the Lord said unto Abraham: 'Get thee out of thy country, and from thy kindred, and from thy father's house, unto the land that I will show thee.' " The religious genius is forever deserting the beaten paths in search of the land God has shown him. To Isaiah all the opinions, all the values, and all the judgments of the world are hopelessly confused and confounded: "Woe unto them who pronounce the evil good and the good evil, who call the bitter sweet and the sweet bitter." What made Socrates prefer hemlock and death rather than life and a betrayal of the god within him? What makes the martyr — the martyr everywhere, all along the frontiers of the spirit — so daring and so fearless? Hanania ben Teradion, Akiba, and their heroic colleagues in our own Jewish tradition, for example? Recall one of the loftiest and one of the most dramatic scenes in the story of our prophets and see how original and how fearless is the man of God.

Jeremiah is facing a royal tribunal. He is charged with speaking treason in times of war. He preached peace when everybody else was shouting war slogans. He denounced the war policies of his king and his country. We read from the Book of Jeremiah. The prosecutor is speaking:

> This man is worthy of death; for he hath prophesied against this city, as ye have heard with your [own] ears. Then spoke Jeremiah unto all the princes and to all the people, saying: "The Lord sent me to prophesy against this house and against this city all the words that ye have heard. Therefore now amend your ways and your doings, and hearken to the voice of the Lord your God; and the Lord will repent Him of the evil that He hath pronounced against you. But as for me, behold, I am in your hands; do with me as is good and right in your eyes. Only know ye for certain that, if ye put me to death, ye will bring innocent blood upon yourselves, and upon this city, and upon the inhabitants thereof; for of a truth the Lord hath sent me unto you to speak all these words in your hearing ears."
>
> (XXVI.11-15)

He does not backwater; he does not speak in ambiguous terms; he does not engage in any stage heroics; he is not sorry for himself; he is simply obeying the word of God.

A *third* characteristic that distinguishes the truly religious, I believe, is one of the gifts we should seek to gain for ourselves as a result of our worship: a certain quietude of mind. Perhaps the word "serenity" describes this. Our rabbinic masters call it *nahat ruah* — composure, peace of mind, emotional stability, mental poise, "a harmonious disposition of the soul," to borrow a phrase from Plato.

Truly religious people are never harassed; they do not despair; they are not in a hurry. "The Lord is with me," they say with the Psalmist, "I shall not fear; what can man do unto me?" He who has faith, says Isaiah, does not make haste. Why this nervous, excited rush? God has all eternity in which to fulfill His purposes. Our times, our purposes, our ambitions are in His hands. In the twenty-third Psalm we have this great boon of religion expressed in lovely form: "Yea, though I walk through the valley of the shadow of death, I shall fear no evil, for Thou art with me."

When all for which he labored was ignored, when his every hope for his people was blasted, Isaiah did not surrender to despair. He saw in it only a temporary setback. In time, his words would be realized. That was as sure as the rising of the sun, for God had spoken them. Therefore, he writes down his message for his people, commits it to his few disciples, and waits — "waits for the Lord." The truly religious "wait for the Lord, wait patiently for Him." That, of course, has been the great boon sensitive men and women have sought in every age.

Please note that it is not passive resignation, much less apathy, that characterizes the truly religious. In contact with a supreme reality, following the light as it is thrown across their paths by the Eternal, they are confident that no final evil can befall them, that no permanent defeat can possibly come upon them, that not even death can undo them. Nature taught John Burroughs this great truth of religion:

> Serene, I fold my hands and wait,
>     nor care for wind nor tide nor sea;
> I rave no more 'gainst time or fate,
>     For lo! my own shall come to me.
> I stay my haste, I make delays —
>     For what avails this eager pace?

I stand amid the eternal ways
And what is mine will know my face.

We can not rush our gardens. We prepare the ground;
we plant and weed and do what needs to be done — and
wait.

"Does Job serve God for naught?" Do we serve God for
naught? No, not for naught. We seek certain gifts, precious
gifts that religion alone can give to them who seek the
Lord. But to be spoiled, pampered darlings of an indul-
ging deity is not our desire; not for the easy and the pleas-
ant do we ask; we do not ask that we be made exceptions
in a universe of law; we do not whine and we do not seek
to escape the inevitable experiences of life. The gifts we
seek are the sense of God's presence — His immediate and
compelling presence that makes us the spokesmen of His
words and the protagonists of all that is eternally just and
everlastingly good; we seek the dauntless courage to be true
to ourselves and to follow our own honorable paths though
we live in a herd; and we seek *nahat ruah* — peace, serenity,
harmony of soul. "In the center of your being, groan not,"
says a Roman sage. A talmudic master, Rabbi Eliezer, expresses it in a classic little prayer.

Do Thy will, O God, in the heavens above, and grant
peace of mind to them who revere Thee below. And do
Thou what is pleasing in Thy sight. Blessed art Thou, O
Lord, who hearest prayer. Amen.

# 7 | THE BLIND SPOT

IN the retina of every man's eye is a point that is not sensitive to light. It is known as the *blind spot*. Objects placed directly under the blind spot are invisible. A coin, for example, held in open view but directly under the blind spot becomes entirely invisible. Every person has a blind spot, though it varies slightly with the individual.

Of recent years, the term *blind spot* has been used in describing localities in which radio reception is poorer than in the surrounding area. Have you ever driven along in your car with the radio functioning properly and suddenly come upon a stretch of the road where the reception turns muffled, if not dead? Once you are out of this area, the radio automatically picks up normal reception. What happened was that you were in a blind spot as far as radio reception is concerned.

What I should like to do is to draw a parallel between the blind spot as we have it in the human eye — or in the air, if you will — and as it is in our spiritual life. Our minds, our understanding, our appreciation of things, of people, of values, have blind spots in them. These blind spots vary with individuals, but all of us have them. We are incapable of seeing certain things; we are incapable of understanding certain things that are clear to others; we have not the capacity to appreciate certain things which are precious to a great many people. It is nothing to be ashamed of. It is simply a limitation of capacities, and every person is limited in some way. God alone is free from these limitations. But we ought to recognize these limitations. Unless we are aware of them, unless we are duly mindful of these blind spots in our mental and emotional makeup, we shall be unjust, we shall be dogmatic, even cruel. Moreover, while we can not remove the blind spots in the retina, we can, if we work at it, control some of the blind spots in our spiritual life.

William James, in an essay on "A Certain Blindness in Human Beings," tells a story of a white traveler among African savages. He had been away from civilization for some time, and was naturally hungry for any bit of news. One day a newspaper came into his possession. He fell to reading it avidly, his eyes glued to that newspaper. The natives watched him. His eyes were fixed on that paper. For the moment nothing else existed for him. When he was through reading it, they offered to purchase the paper from him. He was puzzled. Why should these illiterate natives want the paper? Not one of them could read any language. Why did they want the paper, he asked them. They replied that they wanted it for eye medicine. They saw the physical part of the man; they saw that he had his eyes fixed on that paper and that it pleased him. They had no understanding of print, of communication of thought by symbols or letters on paper. They had no understanding of what was going on in the mind of that man.

James, in the same essay, calls the reader's attention to a dog watching his master reading a book. The dog can not possibly understand what is happening to his master. What comes over him, the dog must speculate, if a dog speculates, that for a long time the master sits still and watches some dead object in his hands? He must be ill. Were he well, he would be running around with him or throwing sticks for him to catch. How can a dog understand the delight an intelligent person experiences from reading a stirring book?

Some years ago, as a student at Hebrew Union College, I was sent to a congregation in Colorado for the High Holy Days. I remember being on the train, going through the prairies of the Mid-West. Miles and miles of flat, rolling prairies greeted the eye as the train sped on its way; there were no hills, no mountains, no rivers — just flat, rich, black soil. I remember commenting to a fellow passenger to the effect that it was monotonous country. The man looked at me, smiled an indulgent smile, and said: "Oh, no; this is very musical country." It was dull and drab and wearisome to me, a city dweller and a theological student; but he was a farmer and knew the worth of rich, black soil. To him it was musical.

Surely you must have heard the judgment passed on wives of certain men: "I don't see what he saw in her to marry her." Perhaps he is intellectual and she is not; perhaps he is especially gifted and she is ordinary. The answer is quite simple: he loves her; therefore he sees and appreciates qualities in her which the casual acquaintance does not see at all.

The blind spot is a sharp reality in our personal lives and in our adjustments. Some things we can not understand, we have not the capacity for it; some conditions we are incapable of recognizing; some situations we are not able to appreciate for the simple reason that we do not have the needed antenna. I have a friend — a brilliant man, head and shoulders above the average man intellectually — who can not tell a brown shoe from a black one, and is likely to go off to work in the morning with a mixed pair of shoes. Shall we find fault with him for it? In every other situation he is brilliant.

Is it rational for a blind person to dismiss color as a hoax, or for a deaf person to dismiss music as a fraud, because he can not see or hear it? Is it rational for a person to sneer at religion as superstition because he has no antenna for religion?

My friends, our personal feuds, our peeves and grudges that corrode and embitter us and ultimately shorten our years are due largely to the blind spots that limit our insights, blur our understanding, cramp our sympathies, and render us not only unlovely but unjust. Awareness of our own blind spots is terribly urgent if we are to flourish as healthy, mature men and women. Awareness, I submit, is the first exercise in mastering our blind spots.

A second exercise I would urge to help us master our blind spots is to seek more impartiality of judgment in those areas of our lives where we feel most intensely. Love *is* blind in many ways. Strong feeling for a certain cause, as for certain people, may blind us to the merits of competing causes and other people.

Why is it that so many parents, for example, are blind to the faults of their own children when they are in competition with other children? Why is the homeliest face God ever permitted to come into the world beauty itself to a doting parent? We must be eternally watchful lest our love for our own — be it our own family, our own religion, our own country — blind us to the virtues of other families, other religions, foreign countries. Family feuds, nationalistic rivalries, religious bigotries are due to many causes; a basic cause is that blind spot in the retina of every man's eye, in every man's mind. The German minister of propaganda recently said, according to a newspaper report, that the meanest German prostitute on the streets of Berlin was a nobler person than any Jewish woman. Here is appalling spiritual blindness that is plunging us into abysmal sorrow.

Third, hands off! We must not play God. No one has enough insight into the life of another to sit in dogmatic judgment upon him. The advice of the Rabbinic sage, spoken some two thousand years ago, is eternally true: "Judge not your neighbor until you have come in ⌐ his place." Henry Thoreau retired to Walden Pond and there lived in solitude. That was his way of realizing what he considered the good life. Walt Whitman loved to travel up and down Broadway, the Bowery, and Brooklyn Bridge on a truck. That was his idea of the good life. May Thoreau condemn Whitman or Whitman condemn Thoreau? Each to his own. Live and let live. Hands off!

Thus may we correct our blind spots, achieve some harmony in our own lives, bring a bit of justice and loving kindness into the lives of all whose lives we touch as we move through the years.

# 8 | BLIND LOYALTIES

I WANT to consider with you this morning the subject of blind loyalties. The winds of blind loyalties have blown out the lamps of reason in large areas of the world. Our own lamps are flickering, and these winds are howling in the night.

We today must rethink our philosophies, reformulate our faith, reshift our values, reorganize the intellectual, moral patterns of our lives as individuals, as groups, as a nation. We are deep in the valley of decision. "Multitudes, multitudes in the valley of decision," our ancient prophet warns us. We must rethink our loyalties. How sane, how valid, are these loyalties that control us?

The forty-second chapter of the Book of Isaiah is classic in our Jewish tradition. It extols the ideal Israel, Israel as the servant of the Lord. Israel finds the true meaning of existence, discovers the highest good for itself and for mankind by dedicating itself as "the servant of the Lord." Israel must remain loyal to this covenant.

The passage was written sometime during the Babylonian exile. In time it goes back about twenty-five hundred years. Who the author of these verses was we do not know. We call him the Second Isaiah, for the reason that his poems were tacked on to the Book of Isaiah.

This passage contains one sentence to which I should like to call your special attention.

"Who is as blind as he that is whole-hearted?" It is a difficult sentence grammatically. It does not lend itself for easy, accurate translation. If you consulted several English versions of this verse, you would find differences in translation. The Hebrew is archaic. Perhaps it has been corrupted by copyists in the course of translation.

We are not interested just now in the accuracy or difficulty of Bible translation as such. We are interested in the human values this verse carries as we have it. "Who is as blind as he that is whole-hearted?"

The ancient prophet-poet touches a human and a common ailment. Today it is at the bottom of much of our sorrows. We see it all around us. Whole-heartedness is often accompanied by a form of spiritual blindness, and this blindness, unless checked, in the end defeats that to which we are whole-heartedly devoted.

I cite a very humble illustration of this truth. I find this illustration of the hurt blind loyalty inflicts in a newspaper account of a drama enacted in the life of a dog. This is the way my morning newspaper reported it:

> Two members of a Somerville dog trio, familar to hundreds of residents of the city as "Three Musketeers," were inseparable even after death took one of them yesterday.
>
> Ted, a four-year old Airedale, refused for nearly an hour to leave his pal, Jerry, a three-legged Alsatian hound, who was fatally injured when struck by a hit-and-run car on the heavily traveled Northern artery. After a policeman enticed Ted far enough from the dying dog to permit a fellow officer to shoot and remove the hound, the Airedale returned to the spot and kept a lonely vigil for another three hours.
>
> Ted and Jerry were jogging along together when they

started across the artery and the three-legged animal was hit. Ted immediately sat beside the other dog and growled and snapped at all comers, both automobiles and pedestrians. Police officers found it impossible to administer aid to the wounded dog. His pal growled and snapped and would not permit anyone to come near him. And after the officers managed to trick the loyal friend away from his wounded comrade, shoot and carry off the mangled dog, the loyal friend returned to the spot where his friend's body was and kept vigil for several hours, till hunger forced him to yield.

Here is superb loyalty. We cannot help but admire it. It is of such stuff that romances are woven, great adventures wrought, heroic lives built, moral qualities developed. Such loyalty captivates our imagination and wins our admiration.

But look closer. This very same superb loyalty only added misery to the stricken animal. It was his friend's loyalty that prolonged his suffering for several hours. It was futile. What was the matter with it? It lacked reason. It lacked the discipline of intelligence.

We must be on guard against blind loyalties, for the reason that blind loyalties defeat themselves. Especially those of us who are whole-hearted — whole-hearted with our children, our friends, our country, our faith — must be on constant guard against a spiritual cataract growing over our eyes and blinding us. "We kill the things we love," Oscar Wilde warns us.

Consider how far-reaching it is in our own lives and in the life of our time.

Few are the parents who are not devoted whole-heartedly to their children. Parents who are heedless of the welfare of their children are the exceptions. The vast majority of parents are loyal, self-sacrificing, whole-heartedly devoted. Have you not observed how some parents ruin their children with the intensity of their love and the absence of mental controls? They cannot see any faults in their children, for the reason that they are *their* children. It is a blind love and a blind loyalty.

From time to time parents will come to me to talk over some school problems of their children. The parents who are responsible, who can be fair, who can see the short-comings of their own children are few. Most of them are blindly partisan. Their children are always right; their children are always fair; their children never distort the truth. It is the school, the teacher, the books, the classmates that are at fault when something goes wrong.

I heard a mother at one of our meetings criticize several Jewish children for what she called certain "Jewish faults." The children were pampered, not always truthful; they were lacking in good sportsmanship. After the meeting she quoted her child as reporting this or that which led to her opinions. I asked her if she thought her child's reports were accurate. She never questioned that, she said. Her child is always fair, always truthful, always thoughtful. Now, I know her child, and I know that she is spoiled, un-reliable, usually unfair. That mother was not dishonest. She was blind to her own. What will be the effects of this blind loyalty in the life of her daughter?

We see the same treacherous tendency in our loyalties to party, race, religion. As a Jew and as a rabbi, I want to note this weakness in Jewish life. Christian ministers might illustrate the same truth with citations from the lives of their congregants.

On the one hand, we have a large number of Jewish folk who have no positive Jewish loyalties. They are far removed from us emotionally and intellectually. They do not know enough, do not care enough, do not feel enough to be upstanding Jewish men and women. They have no inner and no outer ties. They will give some money when an appeal is made which is strong enough to make them personally feel a bit uncomfortable. Once they make their contributions, they feel their Jewish duties have been discharged.

On the other hand, we have a group of people who are ardently Jewish, but are extremely touchy. They are blindly zealous. They see no weaknesses in Jewish life, no faults, no shortcomings. We are a perfect people. They defend everything that goes on in the name of the Jew and Judaism.

Why should we defend faults in Jewish life and character? If we defend every Jewish fault, who will listen to us when we defend ourselves against false charges? Still more, how may we ever improve ourselves if we do not recognize our weaknesses and try to overcome them?

Those men in Jewish history who have exerted the most beneficent influences were outspoken critics, not blind flatterers, of the Jew and Judaism. Surely all of us, as does all the enlightened world, have a profound respect for what the Hebrew prophets have meant in our Jewish development. But these prophets condemned in scathing terms the blind zealots of Judah and Jerusalem.

I cite one example from the writings of these men. Perhaps the greatest among them was Isaiah. At least, he is so regarded by highly competent scholars. He was a citizen of Jerusalem. He loved, his city. For Isaiah, the world centered around Jerusalem. Jerusalem was the center of all his thinking, the object of all his affections. We cannot imagine Isaiah without Jerusalem, no more than we can imagine Dante without Florence. But, with all his intense love for Jerusalem, this is what he said of it, and said over and over again:

How is the faithful city become a harlot! She that was full of justice, righteousness lodged in her; but now murderers.

Thy princes are rebellious, and companions of thieves: every one loveth bribes, and followeth after rewards: they judge not the fatherless, neither doth the cause of the widow come unto them.

(Isaiah 1.21-23)

Who has exerted a larger measure of good, who has endowed the city of Jerusalem and the later centers of Jewish life with more power, more idealism — Isaiah, who lashed his people with sharp, stinging words, or the false prophets, who spoke honeyed words, refusing to see evil anywhere in the life of Judah?

Consider the quality of patriotism as it is functioning in the world today. Much of this patriotism is blind loyalty. It finds its logical expression in the formula, "My country right or wrong." Isaiah's observation, "Who is as blind as he that is whole-hearted?" holds true in the whole-hearted devotion to country.

Blind patriotism it is that has soaked our earth with blood and tears. It is not the critics of the state that have degraded nation after nation; it is the blind patriots. They who cry patriotism loudest may be the most dangerous.

We are living at a time when this is painfully evident. States under dictatorships are based on blind loyalty; they can survive only as long as the masses remain submissive and blind. Why do governments by dictatorship regiment the press, the radio, the school, the church, the forum, the theater, the club? Dictators cannot endure critical appraisal. The masses must repeat what they are told to repeat. They must not reason; they must not question; they must obey — obey, like soldiers in the ranks. That is the tragedy of our time.

Reason is one essential in the refinement of our loyalties — reason, the civilizing agency in the life of man; reason, "the mediating angel between God and man," as one Jewish poet characterized it back in medieval times.

I must place before you at least one more essential in the cultivation of our loyalties. I suggest that it serve as the basic test of their validity. Does our particular loyalty help advance a larger loyalty, or does it abort it? Do our particular loyalties broaden our horizons and deepen our sympathies, or do they restrict our world and narrow our vision?

The Hebrew word for stork is *hasidah,* which means *the kind, the pious* one. At the same time, the stork is classified in Bible tradition with the unclean and forbidden birds. Why? Because, our masters teach us, while the stork is good to its own kind, it has no kindness for outsiders. It is pious and good in terms of a narrow loyalty; hence the Bible brands it as detestable.

Thus, my friends, the words of Isaiah, spoken back in Babylon some twenty-five hundred years ago, hold a message of life and salvation for us. No man is worthy of his human status unless he cherishes loyalties — loyalties to his family, his people, his faith, his highest ideals, his country. But these loyalties must be enlightened. They must be generous. The rays of reason must transfuse them and impregnate them with truth and honor, and a decent respect for the conflicting values other men cherish. And they must be buttressed with personal courage, with the ability to withstand the mob, particularly when the mobs go mad. And mobs are forever going mad. Only when we are intelligent, generous and courageous as well as loyal will our loyalties bless us and those about us.

# 9 | THE STARTING POINT

"THIS is the book of the generations of Adam. In the day that God created man, in the likeness of God made He him. . . ." So reads a Biblical verse, introducing a long and wearisome genealogy. It is the introduction to the "begot" fifth chapter of Genesis, tracing the ancestry of Noah back to Adam. So-and-so lived a hundred years, begot so-and-so, and died. And so on and on for nine generations. On its surface, it is a dry and drab statement. But in the hands of the rabbinic sages it became one of the greatest pronouncements in Judaism; it became one of the master words the Jew has spoken, and the source of a great body of idealism.

The rabbinic teachers translate the verse, "This is the book of the generations of *man*" — of *man* made in the image of God Himself. One of these sages sees in this verse the central principle of the Torah. This book — not the list of dead names of Genesis, chapter five, but the Torah, the Divine Law entrusted to Israel and through Israel to mankind — is meant for human beings. *Ze k'lal gadol batorah,* "This is the major principle of the Torah," says Ben Azai, speaking in the first century. Rabbi Akiba, a generation or two later, countered with the suggestion that the leading principle of the Torah is, rather, the verse, "And you

shall love your neighbor as yourself." Hillel, who lived
several generations earlier, had advanced the opinion that
the whole of the Torah may be reduced to the principle
that is known to us as the Golden Rule, in its negative
version: "What is hateful unto you do not do to another."
These reduce themselves to one major principle. Its im-
portance is far-reaching. The chief concern of the Torah
is man, man the human being, not God in the high heavens, not this or that theology. The Torah is an instrument
meant to discipline, refine, sanctify human life, to achieve
human dignity and human worth in keeping with a divine
pattern. Before the Torah was given to man, say the same
sages, God was in His high heavens, and man was on the
earth below, and between heaven and earth there was no
commerce. The Torah was given to man to serve as a
bridge connecting heaven and earth. The aim of the Torah
is thus: to bring God down to man and to lift man upward
toward God.

Thus the rabbinic teachers see a vital truth in the sentence, "This is the book of the generations of man." But
they do not stop with the assertion that man, the human
being, is the exclusive concern of the Torah. They hurry
to define man. Man is made in the image of God — "in the
likeness of God made He him." Man is an exalted crea-
ture; he holds within himself a breath of the divine. He
walks the earth on two feet, not on four like an animal,
so that he may lift his eyes to the hills, the stars and to
God. In their own quaint way, which sounds strange to
us, the rabbinic teachers observe: "All creatures created
of heaven, both their bodies and souls are heavenly; like-
wise all creatures created of earth, their bodies and their
souls are earthly; with the exception of man, whose soul
is of heaven and whose body is of earth."

I am calling your attention to this verse and to the interpretation our rabbinic teachers have given it because it holds a compelling truth for us today. Here is the starting point in all our social, ethical, political, religious endeavors. We must begin with human beings, work realistically with human nature, and aspire to an exalted human personality fashioned after the image of God Himself. That is the way God is realized on earth — through refined, ennobled, human beings.

An ennobled humanity in terms of refined personalities is not the ideal of our age. We have reduced man to a tool, a blind robot in most instances, a clever and conscienceless monster that flies over cities and drops bombs on innocent people, blowing to dust schools, shrines, hospitals. We have reduced humanity to a goose-stepping Frankenstein, crushing the structures of civilization. Mussolini's twenty-year-old son, I recall reading some time ago, leads a squadron of planes bombing Spanish cities, and his father calls him an idealist. It is in the name of idealism that we mangle helpless human beings — in Normandy, Russia, Poland, the "Western Front." Human worth? Human dignity? A refined, ennobled personality? The ideal is domination, tribalism, lust for power, greed. "The dangerous life" has been placed above the good life. Not ethics, not religion, not reverence for life, but the thrill of smashing every law of God and man and defying heaven and earth in a bombing plane in the clouds is the supreme thrill.

In the light of this mechanized barbarism on the part of gangster nations terrorizing the world, the pronouncement of the ancient rabbinic sages sounds naive, childish, far removed from the world. Yes, the rabbinic doctrine is far removed from the world as it is, and it does sound naive; yet, in this naive sentiment lies the salvation of the world. For here are ethics, here is morality, here is humanity, here is the still small voice.

Are we interested in education? Do we share in the labors of those who would clarify the minds of men, women, children, broaden knowledge, deepen wisdom, and thus extend the frontiers of moral civilization? Are we practically concerned with the lives and well-being of others, perhaps members of our own families, say, our own children? Are we teachers working with impatient minds? Are we social workers seeking to minister to people in need? Are we active in organizations devoted to high purposes?

If we are, we must remember that our starting point is human nature and our ultimate goal is an ennobled human being. Here is the beginning and the end of our idealism. Here, too, is the test of effectiveness and our worth.

That means, first, that we must know human beings. We must understand the stuff of which they are made; we must understand the dreams and the fears that haunt them, the ambitions that drive them, the values that control them, the loves and the hates that impel them.

Perhaps you have had this experience. You drive along in your car, following the road as shown on the map. You discover that you are off the road. You consult your map, and there stated very clearly is the town you wish to reach. The road for you to take is clearly marked. You are desirous of taking that road, but you cannot — and you cannot for the reason that you do not know where you are at the moment. And as long as you do not know where you are, the map is useless, and all the directions are useless. You must find yourself first. Once you have located your own position, the road is clear.

There are said to be five points on the Chinese compass: East, West, North, South, and "where-you-are-now."

We will never be effective as teachers or as parents or as social workers, as friends, as colleagues or as builders of the Golden City unless our starting point is a clear understanding of human nature. A doctor may prescribe accurately but break the morale of his patient by not understanding the foibles, peculiarities, vanities, fears and hopes of his patient.

In the second place, this principle we are considering, as urged by the rabbis, means accepting human nature — not accepting it as fixed and final, but accepting it as a starting point. As parents, as teachers, as friends, as social workers, we must accept human nature as we find it in the same sense in which a physician accepts his patients. The physician does not quarrel with his patients for being sick; he does not upbraid them; he does not fly into righteous indignation because they have acted like idiots; he accepts them as they are and tries to help them.

May I revert to the illustration of the road map? You look at the map and you locate the city for which you are heading. The road between yourself and that city is a poor one. A much better road leads to that city if you were elsewhere. But you are not elsewhere; you are here. It is from *this* point and from this point only that you must travel. All the arguments and all the fretting and fussing in the world will not change the map for you.

We must not only understand human nature but accept it as our starting point. Recently a father boasted to me that he required his fifteen-year-old son to play the violin despite the fact that the boy protested violently. The boy, it seems, had no taste and no aptitude for the violin, and the father's blind insistence turned him all the more against the instrument; but the father was determined that his son be a violinist. Our colleges are crowded with youngsters who are misfits in the halls of learning. They are a drag on the institutions, personally unhappy, wasting their time and their parents' money. We are forcing sparrows to fly like eagles.

This does not mean that we should remain satisfied with mediocrity. We simply accept the limitations of human beings, as a physician accepts his patient, and work for improvement and development.

"This is the book of the generations of man." This religion of ours, if it is to function in the lives of men and community, this social service program if it is to mitigate misery, this job of ours, as parents or teachers — all these have chances for success only if we begin and are appreciative of human nature, with all its foibles, frustrations and capacities. All our problems issue from human needs; all our strivings are to realize human hopes — man defying his earthiness, straining upward.

# 10 | WHEN IS RELIGION REAL?

WHEN does religion cease being mere ritual recited by rote, or mere conventional performance, or mere paper resolutions passed at meetings, or mere socially proper procedure, and become a dynamic, directing the course of our lives, shaping our ideals, determining the moral complexion of our personalities? That is, when does religion become real?

It is important that we reflect on this question from time to time. We are constantly sidetracked from our goals by the tumult of the world. In the realm of religion it is especially easy to get off the main road. Religion is a confused realm; its boundaries are hazy. Highways and side roads crisscross it; many signs are pointing in many directions; contradictory signs are presuming to guide us to the same cities of our hearts' desire. Moreover, in the realm of religion we have a considerable number of thoroughly unreliable guides, who are either riding hobbies, or pushing their own careers, or are blind zealots who know not the lay of the land in its totality. The average person may be completely victimized by pious zealots, especially by those who exploit our fears or pump our vanities.

It is vital that we check our courses from time to time. A good question to put to ourselves is: Is my religion real or is it counterfeit? What makes a religion real, and what makes it false?

The answer is simple. Religion is real when it is personal; it is real when it impinges itself upon our minds and our consciences. It is real when it becomes a gadfly, stinging the lazy conscience into activity. Unless it does disturb the mind and rouse the conscience, unless it does allay our fears and fortify our wills, it is only theoretic religion at best, only a creed recited by rote, only a resolution shouted at a convention, only pious pretense.

A few Biblical instances will help reveal the reality of religion.

The Hebrew Bible does not engage in nice definitions of religion. There is little abstract reasoning in our scriptures. The Bible talks through the lives of men and through specific institutions. The Hebrew prophets have been accepted as the peculiar geniuses of Israel. They have been characterized as the lightning rods that brought the fire of God down to earth. They were men possessed of the divine. Invariably their utterances in the name of God are introduced with the formula, "The word of the Lord came unto me saying . . . ." "Came unto *me*" — came to the individual conscience and stung it into activity. It did not come to a committee, or a convention, or a board of trustees. Isaiah is driven to speak his mind because, as he says, the hand of the Lord rested upon him. He was in the grip of a power beyond himself. He had to obey, with his whole heart and mind. He could not delegate the responsibility to an assistant; he could not do it half-heartedly; he could not do it with any mental reservations. It was too personal and too compelling for any such escape. The same is characteristic of all the prophets. "The Lord God hath spoken, who shall not prophesy?" Amos says in repudiating the suggestion that he ought not speak. Jeremiah confesses in despair:

> If I say: "I will not make mention of Him,
> Nor speak any more in His name,"
> Then there is in my heart as it were a burning fire
> Shut up in my bones,
> And I weary myself to hold it in
> But cannot.

Perhaps the most impressive testimony to the proposition that religion becomes real only as it becomes personal is given in the book of Job. Job was a pious man, but in a worldly sense. He was just, he offered his sacrifices, he was proper in his conduct as in worship. He was a thoroughly upright man, and a thoroughly conventional person. And he prospered. But the visitations of a cruel fate came upon him. His possessions were swept away, his family was murdered, his health broke down. He was sorely afflicted. His friends deserted him; his own wife advised suicide. Painful torments beset him. Why had all this come upon him? Why had God turned against him? Frantically he hurls challenges at God Himself, questioning His justice and His mercy in His dealing with mortal man. Religious he still was, even as he had been all along, though he was speaking many heresies. But out of his physical pain and his spiritual torment, a deeper conception of religion came to him. In the last chapter of the long book of Job — a book that voices bluntly many heresies as well as the pieties of the time — Job, emerging from his awful tribulations, says:

> I had heard of Thee by the hearing of the ear;
> But now mine eye seeth Thee.

Job knew pain, mental as well as physical; he was shaken

out of his superficial, conventional, merely proper religious thought by intense personal experience. Now religion was real — terribly real.

But, some will say, what of the social aspect of religion? Is not religion concerned with the social miseries — with poverty, with crime, with exploitation? War and the terrors of hell are ravaging our lunatic planet. How can we at such a time say that religion is real only when it becomes intensely personal? Did not the prophets concern themselves with the social voices of Israel and Judah?

Yes, of course. The religion that ignores the social issues sells out. It betrays its trust. Its piety then becomes a false front. There is no thought in my mind of evading the social miseries of the day. Prophetic religion is intensely social in its outlook. Read, for example, the seventh and eighth chapters of the Book of Isaiah, and you are impressed with the social sins upon which the prophet calls down the woes of heaven. What are they — greed, exploitation of the helpless, drunkenness, blatant cynicism, arrogant egotism, crowding out the peasant and concentrating the land in the hands of small aristocracy. This is social religion sharply stated.

But the social ideals were personal dynamics. That is the characteristic thing about them. They were not merely resolutions passed at conventions by bored delegates. They burned in the hearts of these prophets. They drove these men of God to distraction. The prophets felt personally responsible for the social sins of their time.

Even history became a personal matter to these angry men of God. Every Israelite was personally present in Egypt, personally served in Pharaoh's brickyards, felt the taskmaster's lash on his own back, though in time he may have been a thousand years removed. So teach our rabbinic sages. We Jews today, when we read our Haggadah, are told that we must place ourselves back in Egypt and feel as if we personally crossed the Red Sea with Moses.

How, then, does religion become real? The answer is by becoming intensely personal. "How shall we make it personal?" you ask.

Religion becomes personal when, first of all, it is sincere. Sincerity transcends everything else in religion. Sincerity defies convention; it ignores personal interests. It becomes personal and real when it becomes, in the words of Jeremiah, "a fire in my bones." I would make sincerity the *primary* test, but not the *only* test.

A second test would be its specific forms of expression. And I do not mean merely in ethical behavior. If our religion is civilized, sincerely professed, it will express itself in conduct, of course. Religion must express itself in specific ritualistic forms as well, if it is to live and function.

Religion is not mere dream stuff; it is not merely "the soul's sincere desire." That is a lovely phrase and holds much truth; but it is not enough, for the reason that religion is not mere sentimentalism. Religion must express itself also in ceremony. We can not rule pageantry out of religion. If we do, we emasculate religion.

Religion was real to our fathers for the reason that it meant a personal discipline. Social ideals became personal responsibilities under Pharisaic law; abstract theologies and abstract ethics became personal, also, through certain ceremonial institutions. Reform Judaism acted violently with ceremonies, and we are paying the price for it with a generation of worship that is stripped naked of its historic forms. A brave attempt is being made today to recover some of the ceremonies we have lost. The sooner we recover them the better.

But these ceremonies must be honest. I am very much concerned about the return of ceremonial to our Reform

Judaism. Ceremonialism must be restored as an honest form of honest worship. There is real danger of ceremonialism being resurrected from an honest grave only to be given a phony pretentiousness. Ceremony must be worship, not theater; it must aim at God, not the galleries. Reverence, not exhibitionism, is the heart of religion.

Our worship in the synagogue and, particularly, in the home must be beautiful in distinctive forms. But the individual life must be touched by the beauty of holiness in its own peculiarly private experiences. Naming a child in the synagogue is a lovely bit of ritual. A new life has come into the world. Why not release the child's name on the wings of a benediction?

We Jews know that circumcision is not a tribal thing, but sealing anew our ancient covenant with our God. The surgeon has been replacing the *mohel*. I have no quarrel with that from a purely surgical standpoint; but why omit the religious service? If we do sterilize the religious significance, then we do reduce the rite to sheer tribalism.

Marriage is something more than a civil contract. The fact that the state has taken over the institution of marriage does not mean that it should become a purely secular contract. Why should marriage anniversaries be only occasions for cocktail parties? Would it not show culture and good breeding and loveliness to mark the happy day with a prayer in the home or in the synagogue?

Much superstition is associated with funerals. Much of the ceremonialism we see enacted is thoroughly primitive and has no place in the lives of cultured modern people. But the solemnity of death and the pathos of final farewells should be experienced in the majesty of sincere worship. *Yahrzeit* is a lovely institution in Judaism. For a year the bereaved recite the *Kaddish* in the synagogue with special thought for their loved departed. Annually they recall the anniversaries of the deaths. *Yahrzeit* has kept the generations together; it has kept alive the lovely and the gracious. Are we growing so "liberal" that we are ignoring even this mark of affection for our own departed? I like the practice of reciting the names of the deceased in the course of our recitation of the *Kaddish*. A considerate, gracious practice of greeting the mourners in the synagogue on their first visit after the death has taken place should be recaptured. We have lost this bit of good manners in the impersonal big plants of the modern "liberal" synagogues.

These are some of the ceremonies in private life we must recapture. They are not to be enacted only on the platforms of our synagogues but in the hearts of our worshippers. That is where religion belongs. That is where it is, if it is real.

We cannot conceive of music without instruments, nor art without forms, nor literature without the vehicles of literary expression — the play, the novel, the essay, the poem. Why do we keep on talking of disembodied religion?

Once we make it personal and give it beauty and integrity of form, it becomes dynamic. Then it becomes real. "When thou walkest it shall lead thee, when thou liest down it shall watch over thee, and when thou awakest it shall talk with thee."

# 11 WHERE THERE IS NO VISION

THE wise man of the book of Proverbs said, many, many centuries ago, "Where there is no vision the people perish." Certainly, that is one of the most universal of truths, and one of the most personal. It is true of nations and true of individuals. This morning I would like to modify his statement a bit: Where there is no vision of the whole, people perish; where there is no vision of the totality of things, men perish. With my bare hand I can wipe out the sun in the heavens; I can eliminate the moon and stars from my vision, by holding it close enough to my eyes. Anything held close enough to one's eyes will wipe out the world; it simply shuts off the vision and destroys perspective. If you wish to view a painting to best advantage, you must view it from a proper distance, or it will be out of proportion. We climb hills and mountains to get a good view of a sunset or a sunrise. Why? Because we want perspective; we want the sweep of the landscape and the horizon.

Perspective means viewing things from a proper distance, appraising them in terms of the whole, in terms of their relationships.

Recently the Central Conference of American Rabbis adopted a new platform, known as "Guiding Principles

of Reform Judaism." Much discussion preceded the adop-
tion of this platform. Various contradictory points of view
had to be harmonized. In the course of these debates,
much criticism was directed against the Pittsburgh Platform, adopted by a group of Reform rabbis in 1885. It
was too liberal, too radical; it had surrendered too much
of tradition; it was not Zionistic enough; it no longer expressed the mind of the Reform Jew. So went the arguments. One of the critics of the Pittsburgh platform made
a penetrating observation. He said that the early Re-
formers had taken a limited view of the hour in Jewish
history. Reform started in the high hopes of the Enlightenment; the Reform fathers were carried away by the
enthusiasm of the liberalism of their day. They failed to
see that the exciting hour would pass and a new restrictive
hour would come. They jumped to the fond hope that the
new day of liberalism that was dawning would never end.
They reformulated Judaism in keeping with permanent
enlightenment in the world. That was the weakness of
their work. They did not prepare for the night. They did
not take the right perspective of their own day.

That, it seems to me, is a shrewd and valid criticism. It
does not reflect on the high-mindedness of the Reform
leaders. It is part of our tragedy, and part of the world's
tragedy, that liberalism miscarried. Better to have dreamed,
worked and failed than not to have seen the vision at all.
And he who has known heights will never again be satisfied with dreary lowlands. But there was an element of
shortsightedness in their thinking.

I am recalling this chapter of our history this morning
because we today are making the same mistake, except
that we are making it in the opposite direction. We are
living in an hour of persecution. No high hope of an
everlasting day of freedom is tantalizing us; the fear of an

endless night of oppression is weighing us down. And the great mistake that we may be committing in our Jewish thinking is that this night will last forever. We, too, are taking a limited, restricted view of the hour — of the dark and bitter hour.

We hear men say — men who should know better — that the emancipation of the Jew from the ghetto has failed, that there is no hope for the Jew in the Western world, that liberalism has miscarried, that the Jew should, therefore, retrench. In fact, it has become quite the style to ridicule the hopes and efforts of the liberals in Judaism of a generation ago, on the ground that liberalism has failed.

Well, liberalism has failed us in large areas of the world; but not everywhere in the world. Besides that, however, let us not take too limited a view of our present troubles. The night will pass and a new day will dawn. If we are to give up liberalism because it has been badly violated, we must, by the same logic, give up the Ten Commandments, because they, too, are constantly violated. Our own government is spending five times as much on fighting crime as it does on education. Shall we, therefore, say that we must abandon ourselves to crime as the rule of life? The vision of peace has failed. A century ago good men dreamed that civilized man had become too rational to engage in war. Victor Hugo wrote: "In the nineteenth century war will be dead, the scaffold will be dead, man will commence to live."* Today, bombers are dumping their cargoes of death on cities jammed with hysterical men and women, blowing up schools, shrines, hospitals. Shall we repudiate forever the vision of peace?

The worst thing that can happen to us is for us to lose

---

* Quoted by Pierre Van Passen, "Days of Our Years," p. 68.

hope. There are goodness, justice and kindness in the hearts of men; there are many, many lovely souls in the world who seek our good. Let us not lose perspective. We Jews today have more outspoken defenders of our rights than we have ever had.

The same need for perspective is urgent in our own congregational life. We are standing at the open door of the year's work.* Our Temple program is just beginning. Our various committees are beginning their work. Urgent as is the immediate practical work, the most important consideration to bear in mind at the very beginning is perspective, is the vision of the whole; unless a clear and valid vision guides us, our work will fail, fail even if it succeeds in the worldly sense. Each department is good only to the extent in which it helps build Jewish religious loyalties through our particular congregation. A thousand people at our meetings preoccupied, however enthusiastically, with matters that have nothing to do with our Jewish religious life and I shall consider the effort a failure; a very small number preoccupied with its legitimate aim of restoring Jews to Judaism and Judaism to Jews, and I shall call it a success.

It is dangerously easy for a school to become so absorbed in its routine, in its office efficiency, in its numbers and crowds that it forgets to teach, and what is the good of it all if it does not teach? It is dangerously easy for a congregation to become absorbed in its hunger for numbers and finances and to forget the reason for its numbers and finances. Where there is no vision the institution perishes; where there is no vision of the whole, where there is no vision of the landscape and the open horizon in our thinking, our causes perish.

---

* Temple Sinai was entering on its second year of existence in 1940.

May I bring the same truth to bear upon our personal lives? Have you not known men and women who were so carried away by the success of the moment that they were entirely undone and finally submitted to despair and failure? They simply could not carry their successes. They assumed that the flush of success would last forever. They forgot — or refused to give heed — that with the days come adversities as well as joys, and that unless a sense of balance and proportion controls us, we shall lose our equilibrium and topple over into failure. I do not know what the statistics are, but many of the divorces are due to a sudden burst of prosperity, which blinded the beneficiaries.

Similarly, the sense of perspective is imperative in the hours of grief. Some of you have surrendered to death a loved one. I have the sad duty of standing by the open grave of your dear one with you. I think I know what that experience has meant.

But would it not be adding pain to our suffering if we persisted in mourning our dead to a point where we made life impossible for the living? We loved our dead, but we love our living ones, too, and they are alive, thank God, and we can do things for them, whereas the deceased are beyond our reach. Would it not be a tragic thing to assume so limited, so restricted a view of our loss, as to bring added suffering upon ourselves and our dear ones?

Lack of perspective on themselves and their world is the major fault with selfish people. They are absorbed with themselves so much that they cannot see the rest of mankind; they love themselves so intensely that they cannot love anyone else; they admire themselves so much that they cannot admire anyone else; they are so greedy, so ambitious for themselves, that they have no consideration for anyone else.

"Where there is no vision the people perish." Would we have the roads of life unfolding before us, with the mountains ahead of us? Would we have a lantern in our hands when the night enfolds us and the paths are obscure? Would we ourselves be a light to others who are following confused paths deep in shadows? Then, let us pray for vision, and discipline our lives with perspective.

# COME, LET US REASON TOGETHER

by Beryl D. Cohon

Foreword by Abram L. Sachar,
*Chancellor, Brandeis University*

Nearly forty years ago, Rabbi Beryl D. Cohon delivered the sermons in this volume to a congregation whose sons were going to war, whose very lives were shattered by the terrible events of the years of the Second World War.

"All the anchors of faith, freedom, democracy, family virtues, religious sanctities were dragging in the storm," Rabbi Cohon wrote, looking back on those years. "We were in dire need of a prophetic word — a word above race, above class, above dogma, above economic determinism, above the despair and cynicism of the day. The Word had to be spoken, however humbly, however inadequately."

Rabbi Cohon's sermons from those dark years shine like beacons across the intervening decades, and speak as clearly to the men and women of today as they did in the shadow of Hitler and the Holocaust. "You and I are living at a time when the world is desperately in need of Isaiah's vision of a rational and just humanity in a rational and just world," he said.

In these beautifully written and inspiring sermons will be found wisdom, strength, vision, and — in the words of Abram L. Sachar in the *Foreword*, written shortly after Rabbi Cohon's death in 1976 — "a passionate appeal to faith and stamina . . . renewed morale in the author's counsel, even in these most disruptive times, 'Come, let us reason together.'"